# SARGENT

# SARGENT

Clare Gibson

BARNES
&NOBLE
BOOKS
NEW YORK

This edition published by Barnes &
Noble Inc., by arrangement with
Saturn Books Ltd.

1997 Barnes & Noble Books

ISBN 0-7607-0044-3

Printed and bound in Singapore

M 10987654321

For Marianne and John Gibson

PAGE 1: **Lord Ribblesdale:**
See page 93

PAGE 2: **Miss Eliza Wedgwood and
Miss Sargent Sketching:**
See page 110

BELOW: **The Misses Vickers:**
See page 52

# CONTENTS

# INTRODUCTION

Rarely has an artist of the caliber of John Singer Sargent been the subject of such extremes of vilification and adulation during his lifetime and after. Standing against every enthusiastic proponent of 'Sargentolatry' was a raging critic, ready to condemn the painter for abusing his outstanding talent by 'pandering' to elitist demands. To this day Sargent's *oeuvre* remains controversial, yet the passage of time has allowed a more objective assessment of the work of a man whom his contemporary, Rodin, described as the 'Van Dyck of our times'.

A highly cultured man, Sargent's cosmopolitan outlook was largely due to the influence of his parents, and to his peripatetic childhood. He was born in Florence on January 12, 1856, to affluent American parents who had traveled to Europe in 1854 to recover from the trauma of the death of their firstborn child. His father, Dr. FitzWilliam Sargent, until 1857 the Attending Surgeon at Wills Hospital, Massachusetts, was descended from English Puritans who had settled in Gloucester, Massachusetts; although the Sargent family boasted a somewhat mediocre artist among its forebears, the main family profession was seafaring.

In contrast, his mother, Mary Newbold Sargent, was the only child of a leather merchant of French lineage. Her generous inheritance enabled the family to remain in Europe, moving with the seasons from fashionable cities to equally sought-after spas. The family (there were four more children after Sargent, of whom only Emily and Violet survived) never returned to America to live, and never established a permanent home. If Dr. Sargent retained some of the Puritanism of his ancestors, his vivacious wife — the leading spirit of the family — was lively, indulgent, and determined to experience European culture to the full. Both parents left their mark on their son, who expressed their contrasting values in his religious murals for the Boston Public Library, and in his more worldly society portraits.

Given the family's life-style, Sargent's early education was, of necessity, varied. Initially his parents taught their son, but as he got older tutors were brought in, and the boy also attended schools in Florence and Dresden. Small wonder, then, that such an informal scholastic background, rather than

ABOVE: *Portrait of Mary Newbold Singer Sargent*,1887. Oil on panel, 10 x 12 in.

RIGHT: *Dr FitzWilliam Sargent*, 1886. Oil on panel, 10 x 12 in.

endowing him with conventional academic skills, developed his general knowledge, his flair for languages, and his love of literature, music and, of course, art. In 1924 William Starkweather summed up the rich cultural mixture that the adult Sargent epitomized: 'an American born in Italy, educated in France, who looks like a German, speaks like an

Englishman, and paints like a Spaniard.' In line with family tradition, Dr Sargent wished his son to join the US Navy, but from an early age Sargent's extraordinary aptitude for art made his choice of career inevitable.

ABOVE: Sargent painting 'en plein air' c. 1885.

RIGHT: Emile Carolus-Duran, *Lady with a Glove*, 1869. Oil on canvas. Sargent learnt the art of society portrait painting from Carolus-Duran.

His mother was a keen sketcher in watercolors, and encouraged her son to draw the many sights that they encountered during their travels. His precocious talent was soon evident, and his mother wrote proudly of her 11-year old son to a relative: '[He] has a remarkably quick and correct eye . . . Thus far he has never had any instruction, but artists say that his touch is remarkable.' It became increasingly apparent that the boy's ability demanded for proper tuition, and his parents accordingly enrolled him in the Accademia delle Belle Arti in Florence. The move proved an unhappy experience, and prompted an exploratory family visit to Paris to see if their son's skills would be better developed in this renowned center of artistic excellence. There Sargent and his father offered the boy's portfolio for the inspection of the prominent portraitist Emile-Auguste Carolus-Duran (1838-1917), who pronounced that, although Sargent had 'much to unlearn', he showed 'promise above the ordinary', and accepted him as a student in October 1874.

In a striking parallel to his young pupil, Carolus-Duran came to be regarded as an accomplished painter who had succumbed to the seductive lure of society portraiture. In the 1860s a painter of the Realist style, by the 1870s he was ordering his students to emulate the Spanish master of light and tone: 'Velázquez, Velázquez, Velázquez, study Velázquez without respite.' He established his atelier in 1872 and accepted about 20 predominantly English and American pupils, visiting them twice a week to monitor their progress. He was a rigorous tutor, insisting that his students paint directly onto the canvas without making any preliminary sketches or underpainting, and without any subsequent reworking. Thus every brushstroke had to be crucial to the painting and perfectly executed. In this disciplined atmosphere, Sargent learned the techniques of oil painting fast, but felt the need to supplement his studies in the drawing class of Professor Adolphe Yvon at the École des Beaux-Arts.

ABOVE: Robert Louis
Stevenson: *Two Figures*,
1885. Pencil on paper,
9¹⁄₁₆ x 13⁵⁄₁₆ in.

RIGHT: Unfinished version of
*Madame Pierre Gautreau*.
See also page 49.

By 1877 Emily Sargent noted that her brother was
working 'like a dog from morning to night'; the young
man's efforts, however, were starting to earn
recognition. As well as assisting Carolus-Duran in a
ceiling decoration for the Musée du Luxembourg, in
this year he exhibited at the Paris Salon for the first
time, showing his portrait *Miss Frances Sherborne
Ridley Watts*. Anxious for the Salon-goers' approval, in
the summer he holidayed in Brittany, with the
intention of preparing a genre painting of the type
then fashionable. The trip resulted in an Honorable
Mention at the Salon in 1878 for *Oyster Gatherers of
Cançale*, a success which he equaled the following
year with a portrait of Carolus-Duran. Sargent's
depiction of his mentor brought him six portrait
commissions and set him on the path to fame. In the
early 1880s a string of increasingly unconventional
portraits shown at the Salon — *Madame Edouard
Pailleron, The Pailleron Children, Dr Samuel Jean Pozzi
at Home, The Lady with the Rose, The Daughters of
Edward Darley Boit,* and *Mrs Henry White* — would
establish his reputation as an accomplished and
inventive portrait painter.

By the late 1870s Sargent felt secure enough as an

artist to leave Paris for numerous trips to other
countries, both to further his studies, and to gather
'primitive' genre material. In 1878 he visited Capri,
where he painted a beautiful Capri girl in various
Mediterranean settings. 1879-80 Sargent spent in
Spain, paying homage to Velázquez at the Prado and
drinking in the heady Iberian atmosphere, and in North
Africa, capturing the area's exoticism in masterly
watercolors such as *Fumée d'Ambre Gris* (1880). The
year 1880 saw him in the Netherlands, studying the
work of Frans Hals, whose spearlike brushstroke
Sargent later incorporated into his repertoire, and in
Venice, which he revisited throughout his life. Inspired
by the city's haunting quality, he produced a number
of Venetian watercolors whose subtle, shadowy
qualities were not appreciated by an unimpressed
audience, which condemned them as being gloomy
and degraded. Acclaim came, however, with a genre
painting first conceived during his trip to Spain: *El
Jaleo: Danse des Gitanes* (1882). This large canvas, in
which Sargent acknowledged his debt to both
Velázquez and Goya, portrayed an Andalusian Gypsy
dancing a passionate flamenco, and met with
universal approval.

Emboldened by his success, Sargent now cast
about for a suitable subject with which to create a
triumph at the Salon, and in Madame Pierre Gautreau
he believed that he had found it. The wife of a
wealthy banker, Virginie Gautreau was a society
beauty whose ostentatious presence fascinated all
who met her. So anxious was Sargent to paint her that
he waived his fee and spent a frustrating summer in
Brittany 'struggling' with her 'unpaintable beauty and
hopeless laziness'. The resultant portrait, exhibited in
1874, was indeed a sensation, but its effect
completely backfired. Madame Gautreau's idol-like
stance, liberal use of cosmetics, and the fallen
shoulder strap of her dress, horrified critics and public
alike — 'She looks decomposed,' lamented Ralph
Curtis — to the extent that her mother begged
Sargent to withdraw the picture which had made her
daughter a laughingstock. The unfortunate debacle
was summed up by *Academy*: '[Sargent's] intention,
no doubt, was to produce a work of absolutely novel
effect — one calculated to excite, by its *chic* and
daring, the admiration of the ateliers and the
astonishment of the public. And in this the painter has
succeeded beyond his desire.'

Deeply upset by this humiliation, Sargent even
considered giving up painting; instead he moved to
London. He had exhibited there in 1882, and in 1884
he had spent time in England painting members of the
Vickers family and Robert Louis Stevenson. In 1885
he wrote to a friend: 'I am rather out of favor . . . in
Paris . . . There is perhaps more chance for me [in

LEFT: Claude Monet, *Woman with Parasol*, 1886. Oil on canvas 51½ x 34⅝ in. Sargent met Monet in 1876 and felt a close affinity with him, admiring his work greatly.

ABOVE: *Self-portrait*, 1892. 51½ x 34½ in.

RIGHT: Study of drapery for *The Frieze of the Prophets*, c. 1892. Charcoal and white chalk, 24⅜ x 18¹⁄₁₆ in.

FAR RIGHT: Detail from *The Frieze of the Prophets* in the Boston Public Library. The figures are Amos, Nahum, Ezekiel, Daniel and Elijah.

London] as a portrait painter.' In 1886 he finally quit Paris for London, although he continued to exhibit uncontroversial portraits at the Salon and, in 1889, was named a *chevalier* of France's Legion of Honor. Although he would establish a studio in London, he spent the summer of 1885 at Broadway — an artists' colony — on the River Avon; Fladbury Rectory and Calcot, where he settled his family, also became favorite haunts. Here he painted works which came very close to being Impressionist.

In Paris, Sargent had become acquainted with many leading Impressionists, and felt a close affinity with Monet, whom he had first met in 1876. He admired Monet's work greatly, and stayed at Giverny in 1887 to watch him at work, and to paint *en plein air* himself; *Claude Monet Painting at the Edge of a Wood* (1887-89) was a notable result of the visit. Yet although Sargent was fascinated by the Impressionists' treatment of light, he never fully adopted their strict ethos. Monet later recalled Sargent's visit: 'I gave him my colors and he wanted black, and I told him, "But I haven't any." "Then I can't paint," he cried, and added, "How do you do it?"' Despite painting many landscapes and depictions of bourgeois life that were reminiscent of the Impressionists' style, Sargent was never accepted by

the avant-garde: Pissaro dismissed him as 'an adroit performer', while Monet himself later denied that Sargent was ever an Impressionist, saying: 'He was too under the influence of Carolus-Duran.'

Once committed to England, Sargent was involved in founding the New English Art Club in 1886, a society whose aim was to marry English artistic feeling with French Impressionist techniques. In the English landscapes that he painted for relaxation, Sargent displayed many of the club's principles. Attractive English riverside scenes, such as *A Boating Party* (c1889) and *Paul Helleu Sketching with his Wife* (1889), were painted with an Impressionistic fluidity and awareness of color, but also with the tonal contrasts and modeling of form that the French avant-garde abhorred. It was with a quintessentially 'English

Impressionist' painting — *Carnation, Lily, Lily, Rose* (1885-87) — that Sargent re-established his reputation. The picture took nearly two years to paint, as Sargent only worked on it for a few minutes each evening when the light was exactly right. Taking its title from a popular song, the painting showed Dorothy and Polly Barnard lighting Japanese lanterns in a garden strewn with lilies and roses. It's delightful subject and luminous effect charmed the English, and it was bought for the nation. Despite its appeal, however, some detractors damned the picture as being an Anglicized, sentimentalized example of inferior 'Salon Impressionism'.

In England, Sargent resumed his bread-and-butter work of portraiture. At first, English critics appeared unimpressed with his work. *Mrs Frederick Barnard*

RIGHT: Asher Wertheimer, c. 1898. Black and white sketch.

RIGHT: Bronze Crucifix, c. 1889. 44 x 31 x 3 in.

was shown at the first New English Exhibition in 1886 to muted acclaim, but The Misses Vickers (1886) was both voted 'worst picture of the year' by visitors to the Royal Academy, and witheringly condemned as being 'clever' by the critics. A different view of his talents was taken in the land of his forefathers, however.

In 1887 Sargent was invited to America to paint the portrait of Elizabeth Allen Marquand; this was his second visit (he had first traveled to the United States in 1876 to claim his American citizenship in accordance with United States law). In Boston he received many further commissions, and soon became widely fêted, his lionization resulted in society portraits such as Isabella Stewart Gardner (1888) and Mrs Edward D. Boit (1888). The Boston Transcript summed up the appeal of his portraits to genteel Boston society, as displaying 'the presence of real people whose appearance vouches for their excellent breeding and antecedents'. In New York Sargent painted the Vanderbilt family and Mrs Adrian Iselin in 1888. Such was his success that he returned to America in 1889 and 1890. Sargent evidently found

his welcome in the United States inspiring, for in 1890 two American paintings — La Carmencita, a charming rendition of a popular Spanish dancer, and the dignified Mrs Edward L. Davis and her Son Livingston — earned him widespread critical approval on both sides of the Atlantic.

It was this latter portrait in particular, along with the elegant and assured Lady Agnew of Lochnaw (1892-93), that helped popularize Sargent's work in England, and prompted the rich and famous to beat a path to his Tite Street studio in the hope of immortalization. At the start of the 1890s, however, his reputation was as yet unconsolidated, and he therefore undertook non-commissioned portraits in order to demonstrate his ability to a wider audience. A striking example of this policy was Ellen Terry as Lady Macbeth (1889), a dramatic depiction of the great actress which William Walton described as 'a portrait and a drama, both at once'. Yet neither this painting, nor later portraits of the mid-1890s such as Miss Elsie Palmer (1889-90), Coventry Patmore (1894) or W. Graham Robertson (1894), received unqualified praise — even from the

subjects. W. Graham Robertson described a sitter's ambivalent attitude toward Sargent's unerringly accurate, but occasionally unflattering work: 'It is positively dangerous to sit to Sargent. It's taking your face in your hands.'

Yet by the late 1890s, by which time he had been elected RA (1897), Sargent's exalted stature was undeniable, thanks to the impact of his portraits of members of the Wertheimer family, and enchanting works such as *Mrs Carl Meyer and her Children* (1896), *The Wyndham Sisters* (1899) and the informal *Mr and Mrs Isaac Newton Phelps Stokes* (1897). Sargent now found himself in a position to demand that his subjects sit in his Chelsea studio, regardless of their proximity to London, and that they pay a fee of 1,000 guineas ($5,000) for the honor. Such was the prestige of a Sargent portrait, however, that even Americans made the long trip.

Sargent's society portraits recall those of Joshua Reynolds (1723-92), Thomas Gainsborough (1727-88) and Thomas Lawrence (1769-1830), and his main patrons were inevitably wealthy plutocrats and aristocrats, who were painted in the full trappings of privilege, leading Roger Fry to comment dryly in 1900: 'Such works must have an enduring interest to posterity simply as perfect records of the style and manners of a particular period.' Certainly portraits such as *The Sitwell Family* (1900), *Lord Ribblesdale* (1902) and *Sir Frank Swettenham* (1904) reveal their subjects' almost chilling upper-class arrogance, but they also create a fascinating illusion of glamour and refinement. Sargent was no seeker after fame, however: he declined King Edward VII's offer of a knighthood in 1907, and also the opportunity to paint the monarch's coronation portrait in 1901. A shy man, he preferred to exchange the limelight for his privacy.

Sargent's work rate was phenomenal: between 1895 and 1899 he showed 24 portraits at the Royal Academy, and between 1900 and 1907 he produced between 15 and 25 portraits a year. Indeed, during a trip to America in 1903 he painted 20 portraits alone, including the likeness of President Theodore Roosevelt. Unsurprisingly, by 1896 Sargent was becoming disenchanted with his relentless diet of portraiture. In 1907 he professed himself 'sick and tired of portrait painting', and decided, while painting his self-portrait for Florence's Uffizi Gallery, that enough was enough. Yet, unable to resist the anguished pleading of would-be sitters such as Winston Churchill and Nijinsky, he compromised by dashing off portrait drawings in charcoal in a single sitting, for which he charged $400. In the last 25 years of his life he reluctantly produced no less than 600 of these, and after 1907 only rarely succumbed to requests for portraits in oil.

ABOVE: Cartoon of Sargent by Max Beerbohm, c. 1900. Graphite, pen and wash. 16 x 8½ in.

RIGHT: *Mrs Siddons* by Sir Thomas Lawrence, 1804. Sargent's work recalled that of Royal paintes Sir Joshua Reynolds and his successor, Lawrence.

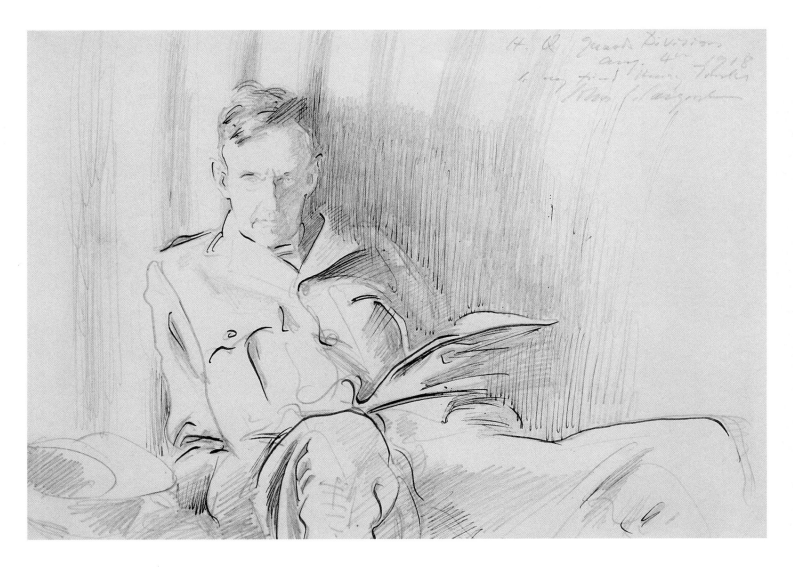

Despite occasional lapses, from 1907 Sargent was resolved to devote his full attention to work of an altogether less worldly nature, and henceforth 'to paint nothing but Jehovah'. During his trip to America in 1890, friends had proposed Sargent as an ideal candidate to decorate part of the upper hall of the new Boston Public Library. It was envisaged that this grand civic building would epitomize the principles of a style which would subsequently be dubbed 'the American Renaissance'. Despite Sargent's relative lack of experience with murals, fellow commissionee Edwin Austin Abbey hastened to reassure those who doubted his suitability for the task: 'He can do *anything* . . . and the Boston people need not be afraid that he will be eccentric or impressionistic.' Relishing this escape from portraiture, Sargent accepted the invitation, and settled on the history of religion as the theme up on which he would base his decorations for the opposing ends of the hall: one extremity would represent paganism and Judaism, while its counterpart would be a stirring tribute to Christianity.

His childhood friend Vernon Lee once observed that Sargent was fascinated by the 'bizarre and outlandish'. His new venture gave him reason to research both in detail, and he traveled to Egypt, Athens, Istanbul and Jerusalem — the cradle of some

ABOVE: Sir Henry Tonks, 1918. Pencil and ink on paper. 9¾ x 14⅝ in.

RIGHT: Study for *Gassed*, 1918-19. Charcoal and stump on paper, 18½ x 24½ in.

of the world's most important religions — during 1890 and 1891. There he made field trips to many ancient sites, feverishly sketching the indigenous architecture, ornamentation, and people, in order to capture on paper as many authentic touches as he could. Back in England, over the following three years he retreated to the solitude of his studio in Abbey's country home to incorporate these details into his murals. The work progressed painfully slowly, for Sargent was now at the height of his fame as a portraitist, and consequently in constant demand in London.

By 1895, the year in which the library opened, Sargent had completed only two sections of the pagan end: a lunette depicting the persecuted Israelites and a ceiling painting of a pantheon of pagan gods. That Sargent had drawn upon the work of other artists was clear: the influence of Michaelangelo, Tiepolo, the Pre-Raphaelites and the Symbolists, as well as Yvon, was unmistakeable. This eclectic, and perhaps overly dramatic style was, however, fully in

the conventions of the American Renaissance. Both works were exhibited at the Royal Academy in 1894, eliciting an astounded response from the *Saturday Review*: 'We are much too startled to comprehend . . . how the realistic painter of so many mundane portraits has suddenly become the illustrator of Ezekiel.' While supervising the installation of these and the *Frieze of the Prophets* in Boston, Sargent received a further commission for a scheme to connect the ends of the hall. In 1903 the works which made up the Christian end — *Frieze of the Angels, The Trinity* and a remarkable three-dimensional crucifix, in which Adam and Eve share Christ's death agonies — were at last put in place. The final series of murals, including *Our Lady of Sorrows*, was installed in 1916, but the linking scheme not until the next year.

Sargent often referred to his Boston work as his 'white elephant', but his patrons were delighted with it, and in 1916 he was asked to create the decorations for the rotunda of Boston's neoclassical Museum of Fine Arts, a project which would occupy him for the rest of his life. Given a free hand, he took full advantage of the trustees' liberality, even going so far as to remodel the rotunda itself. In 1921 the work was

finished, and the trustees were so impressed by Sargent's medallion-like paintings, whose subjects were either allegories or drawn from classical mythology, that they asked him to carry them over to the main staircase; he finished this undertaking in the year of his death.

Despite general American approval of his work, European commentators mainly ignored the Boston murals. On Sargent's part, it is tempting to see them as an expression of his civic responsibility rather than of any passionate belief.

From 1900, Sargent escaped the conflicting demands of portraiture and mural painting by traveling. Accompanied by a small band of friends and relations, he took refuge in beautiful locations such as Venice, where he sketched from a gondola or recorded the pure lines of classical objects. Not all his subjects were so predictable, however: in 1911 the Carrara marble quarries, for example, proved of endless fascination to him. On these relaxed vacations Sargent made thousands of watercolors *en plein air*, capturing both static landscapes, and his companions in informal poses. Watercolor painting became an increasingly important medium of expression for

Sargent, and in 1904 he joined the Royal Society of Painters in Watercolors, with whom he exhibited until his death. As his watercolor technique matured, Sargent would typically make a meticulous pencil drawing and overlay it with broad brushstrokes to create a sparkling, tightly composed, tonal painting. Although a master of resist and impasto techniques, his strength lay in his faultless draftsmanship and confident touch. Yet despite the virtuosity of many of his watercolors, such as *Isabella Stewart Gardner* (1922), neither Sargent nor his critics took his work in this medium seriously, the photographer Paul Strand complained in 1922: 'He gives us merely . . . the average vision of the travel-book illustrator — a record of something that has been seen rather than life that has been felt.'

It was during a painting trip in the Austrian Tyrol that Sargent was stranded for three months on the outbreak of World War 1. Apart from this minor inconvenience, Sargent managed largely to ignore the conflict until the death of his niece in Paris in 1918. In May of the same year he received a letter of invitation from the British prime minister, Lloyd George, to paint 'the fusion of British and American forces'. In July 1918, therefore, accompanied by Henry Tonks, he set off for war-torn France, where he camped with the Guards Division near Arras. Here he made many watercolor sketches of his surroundings, which suggest his apparent emotional detachment. A suitable subject for an 'epic' eluded him, until he finally returned to England in October, having settled on 'a harrowing sight, a field full of gassed and blindfolded men' that he had witnessed at le-Bac-du-Sud; *Gassed* was completed in 1919. Applying the same compositional principles that he had used in *The Frieze of the Prophets*, Sargent's procession of maimed and stumbling soldiers — 'golden-haired Apollos . . . with bandages over their eyes,' as E. M. Forster described them — was a moving testament to the pity of war. Named picture of the year in 1919, the impact of *Gassed* was such that many people fainted at the sight of it. Sargent later undertook further military-related commissions, but neither his group portrait, *Some Officers of the Great War* (1920-22), nor the two memorial paintings that he painted in 1922 for Harvard University's Widener Library, came anywhere close to the tragic lyricism of *Gassed*.

Sargent died peacefully in London in April 1925. Buried in Woking, England, he was honored with a memorial service at Westminster Abbey, and exhibitions over the following year in London, Boston, and New York. He had produced nearly 600 portraits in oils, 1,600 watercolors, and over 600 landscapes and genre paintings in oils. Yet even after his death the controversy continued as to his artistic importance. Aficionados considered him a modern Old Master; his critics condemned his 'dullness and propriety' (Whistler), and pronounced his work 'artificially antique, a cold and soulless eclecticism' (Forbes Watson). His wealthy patrons loved him because he 'showed them to be rich' (Osbert Sitwell), but Roger Fry commented that his art 'applied to social requirements and social ambitions'; anyone of inferior social status was represented as merely part of the scenery. The main criticism leveled at Sargent was that of superficiality, an accusation which haunted him, leading him to protest, 'I do not judge, I only chronicle', and to remark sadly: 'Very few writers give me credit for the insides, so to speak.' Yet he was a master of social nuance and sensitivity, capturing his subjects' preoccupations with deceptive ease and consummate skill. And in the end, Sargent was one of the last artists to understand pre-modern artistic conventions, employing them in subtle synthesis with many avant-garde elements to create a bravura style that was totally his own — a style that is only now being accorded the appreciation that it deserves.

ABOVE RIGHT: The ceiling of the rotunda showing Sargent's decorations.

RIGHT: Sargent's studio, 31 Tite Street, London. Photograph c. 1920.

**Two Wine Glasses** c.1875
Oil on canvas, 18 x 14½ in.
Private Collection/Bridgeman Art Library, London

**Rehearsal of the Pasdeloup Orchestra at the Cirque d'Hiver** 1876
Oil on canvas, 21¾ x 18¼ in.
Charles Henry Hayden Fund,
Museum of Fine Arts,
Boston, MA

**The Oyster Gatherers of Cancale** 1877
Oil on canvas, 16¼ x 23¾ in.
Gift of Mary Appleton (35.708),
Museum of Fine Arts,
Boston, MA

**Head of a Girl from Capri** 1878
Oil on canvas, 17 x 12 in.
Private collection/Bridgeman Art Library, London

**Capri** 1878
Oil on canvas, 30¼ x 25 in.
Bequest of Helen Swift Neilson
Museum of Fine Arts,
Boston, MA

**Sir Philip Sassoon** 1923
Oil on canvas, 37½ x 22¾ in.
Tate Gallery, London

**Madame Edouard Pailleron** 1879
Oil on canvas, 82 x 39½ in.
The Corcoran Gallery of Art, Museum purchase
Washington, DC

**Woman with Furs** c.1880
Oil on canvas, 11⁵⁄₁₆ x 8¾ in.
© Sterling and Francine Clark Art Institute,
Williamstown, MA

**Fumée d'Ambre Gris** 1880
Oil on canvas, 54¾ x 35 ¹¹⁄₁₆ in.
© Sterling and Francine Clark Art Institute,
Williamstown, MA

**The Pailleron Children (Edouard and Maire-Louise)**
1881
Oil on canvas 60 x 69 in.
Purchased with funds from the Edith M. Usry Bequest in
Memory of her parents Mr. and Mrs. George Franklin Usry, the
Dr. and Mrs. Peder T. Madsen Fund and the Anna K. Meredith
Endowment Fund, 1976.61.
Des Moines Art Center, IA

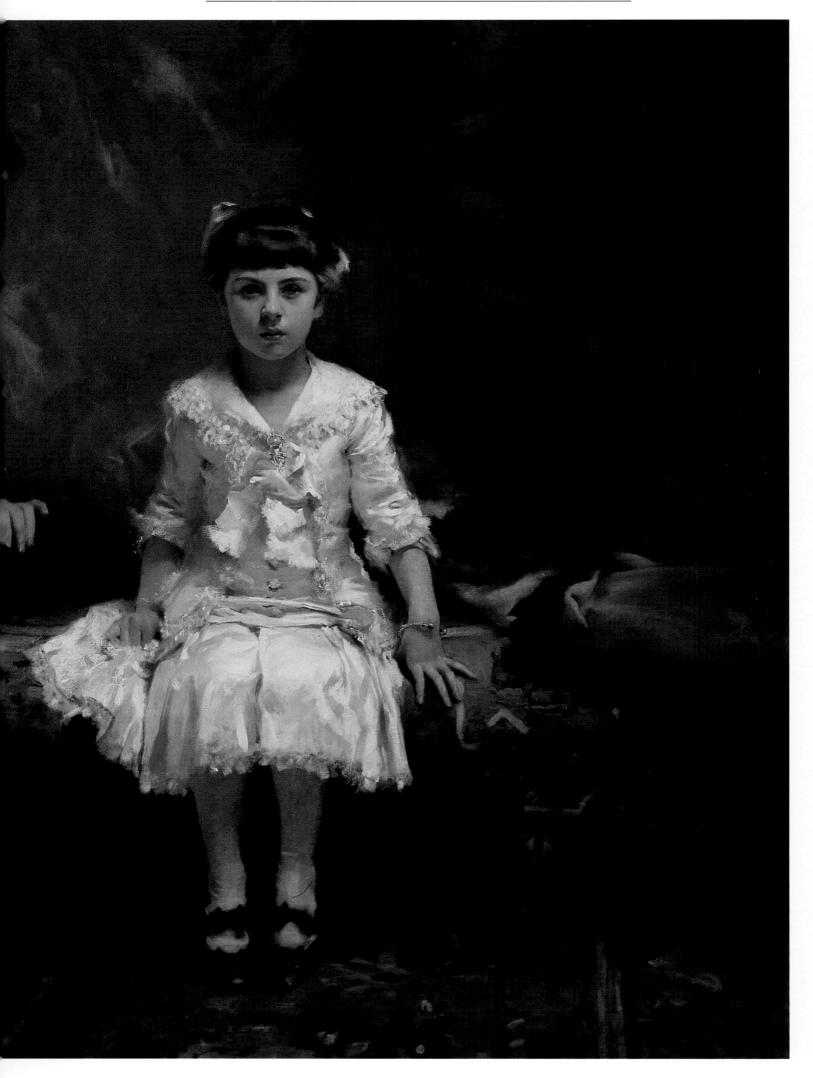

**Dr. Pozzi at Home** 1881
Oil on canvas, 80½ x 44 in.
The Armand Hammer Collection, UCLA at the Armand Hammer
Museum of Art and Cultural Center, Los Angeles, CA

**El Jaleo** 1882
Oil on canvas, 94½ x 137 in.
Isabella Stewart Gardner Museum,
Boston, MA

**The Daughters of Edward D. Boit,** 1882
Oil on canvas 87 x 87 in.
Gift of Mary Louisa Boit, Florence D. Boit, Jane Hubbard
Boit and Julia Overing Boit in memory of their father
Edward Darly Boit
Museum of Fine Arts,
Boston, MA

**Street in Venice** 1882
Oil on wood, 17¾ x 21¼ in.
Gift of the Avalon Foundation,
National Gallery of Art,
Washington, DC

**Palazzo Labia, Venice**
Oil on canvas.
Private collection/Bridgeman Art Library, London

**Portrait of Mrs. Daniel Sargent Curtis (Ariana Randolf Wormeley)** 1882
Oil on canvas, 28 x 21 in.
Spencer Museum of Art, University of Kansas:
Samuel H. Kress Study Collection, 60.59

**Venice Par Temps Gris** c. 1882
Oil on canvas 20 x 27 in.
National Trust,England/
Bridgeman Art Library, London

**Mr. and Mrs. John White Field**  1882
Oil on canvas, 44 x 33½ in.
John Wm. and Eliza Field Collection
The Pennsylvania Academy of the Fine Arts, Philadelphia, PA

**Madame X (Madame Pierre Gautreau)** 1884
Oil on canvas, 82¼ x 43¼ in.
The Metropolitan Museum of Art,
Arthur Hoppock Hearn Fund, 1916. (16.53)

**Garden Study of the Vickers Children** c. 1884
Oil on canvas, 54³⁄₁₆ x 35⅞ in.
Gift of the Viola E. Bray Charitable Trust,
The Flint Institute of Arts, Flint, MI

**Auguste Rodin** 1884
Oil on canvas, 28¾ x 20⅞ in.
Musée Rodin,
Paris

**The Misses Vickers** 1884
Oil on canvas 54 x 72 in.
Sheffield City Art Galleries,
England/Bridgeman Art Library, London

**Reapers Resting in a Wheatfield** 1885
Oil on canvas, 28 x 36 in.
The Metropolitan Museum of Art,
Gift of Mrs. Francis Ormond, 1950. (50.130.14)

**The Breakfast Table** 1884
Oil on canvas, 21¾ x 18¼ in.
Bequest of Grenville L. Winthrop,
Harvard University Art Museums
Cambridge, MA

**Carnation, Lily, Lily, Rose** 1885-86
Oil on canvas, 68½ x 60½ in.
Tate Gallery,
London

**Fête Familiale: The Birthday Party** 1887
Oil on canvas, 24 x 29 in.
The Ethel Morrison and John R. van Derlip Funds
The Minneapolis Institute of Arts, MN

**A Lady and a Little Boy Asleep in a Punt Under the Willows** 1887
Oil on canvas, 22 x 27 in.
Calouste Gulbenkian Museum,
Lisbon, Portugal

**Elizabeth Allen Marquand (Mrs. Henry G. Marquand)** 1887
Oil on canvas, 169 x 107 in.
Gift of Eleanor Marquand Delanoy,
The Art Museum, Princeton University, NJ

**Robert Louis Stevenson** 1887
Oil on canvas, 20 x 24⅓ in.
Bequest of Mr. and Mrs. Charles Phelps Taft,
The Taft Museum,
Cincinnati, OH

**Claude Monet Painting at the Edge of a Wood** 1887-89,
Oil on canvas, 21¼ x 25½ in.
Tate Gallery,
London/Bridgeman Art Library, London

**Dennis Miller Bunker Painting at Calcot** 1888
Oil on canvas mounted on masonite, 27 x 25¼ in.
Daniel J. Terra Collection, 36.1980
Photograph © 1996 Courtesy of Terra Museum of American Art,
Chicago, IL

**Lady Fishing – Miss Ormond** 1889
Oil on canvas, 72¾ x 38½ in.
Tate Gallery,
London

**A Boating Party** c. 1889
Oil on canvas, 34⅝ x 36⅜ in.
Gift of Mrs. Houghton P. Metcalf in memory of her husband Houghton
P. Metcalf
Museum of Art, Rhode Island School of Design, Providence, RI

**Paul Helleu Sketching with his Wife** 1889
Oil on canvas, 26⅛ x 32⅛ in.
The Brooklyn Museum, NY/Bridgeman Art Library, London

**The Rialto, Venice**
Oil on canvas, 17¾ x 21¼ in.
Private Collection/Bridgeman Art Library,
London

**Ellen Terry as Lady Macbeth** 1889
Oil on canvas, 87 x 45 in.
Tate Gallery,
London

**Miss Priestley** c. 1889
Oil on canvas, 36 x 25 in.
Tate Gallery,
London

**La Carmencita** 1890
Oil on canvas, 90 x 54½ in.
Musée Franco-Americaine Blerancourt Chauny, Giraudon/Bridgeman Art Library, London

**Mrs. Edward L. Davis and Her Son Livingston** 1890
Oil on canvas, 86 x 48 in.
Frances and Armand Hammer Purchase Fund,
Los Angeles County Museum of Art, CA

**Head of an Arab** c. 1891
Oil on canvas, 31½ x 23¼ in.
Gift of Mrs. Francis Ormond, the artist's sister,
Museum of Fine Arts,
Boston, MA

**Sketch of Santa Sofia** c. 1891
Oil on canvas, 31½ x 24¼ in.
The Metropolitan Museum of Art,
Gift of Mrs. Francis Ormond, 1950. (50.130.18)

**George Nathaniel, Marquis Curzon of Kedleston** 1890
Oil on canvas, 39⅓ x 30¾ in.
Royal Geographical Society, London/Bridgeman Art Library, London

**Lady Agnew of Lochnaw** 1892-93
Oil on canvas 49 x 39¼ in.
National Gallery of Scotland, Edinburgh/Bridgeman Art Library, London

**Elizabeth Winthrop Chanler (Mrs. John Jay
Chapman)** 1893
Oil on canvas, 49⅜ x 40½ in.
Gift of Chanler A. Chapman
National Museum of American Art,
Smithsonian Institution, Washington, DC/ Art Resource, NY

**Coventry Patmore** 1894
Oil on canvas, 36 x 24 in.
National Portrait Gallery,
London

**Interior in Venice,** 1899
Oil on canvas, 25½ x 31¾ in.
Royal Academy of Art, London/
Bridgeman Art Library, London

**W. Graham Robertson** 1894
Oil on canvas, 90 ¾ x 46 ¾ in.
Tate Gallery,
London

**Mr. and Mrs. Isaac Newton Phelps Stokes** 1897
Oil on canvas, 84¼ x 39¾ in.
The Metropolitan Museum of Art,
Bequest of Edith Minturn Phelps Stokes (Mrs. I. N.), 1938. (38.104)

**Asher Wertheimer** 1898
Oil on canvas, 58 x 38½ in.
Tate Gallery, London/
Bridgeman Art Library, London

**The Wyndham Sisters: Lady Elcho, Mrs. Adeane, and Mrs. Tennant** 1899
Oil on canvas, 115 x 84⅛ in.
The Metropolitan Museum of Art,
Catharine Lorillard Wolfe Collection, Wolfe Fund, 1927. (27.67)

**Rio di San Salvatore, Venice** c. 1900-08
Watercolour and graphite, 10 x 13½ in.
Isabella Stewart Gardner Museum,
Boston, MA

**The Sitwell Family** 1900
Oil on canvas, 67 x 76 in.
Private collection/Bridgeman Art Library, London

**Ena and Betty, Daughters of Asher and Mrs Wertheimer** 1901
Oil on canvas, 73 x 51½ in.
Tate Gallery,
London

**Lord Ribblesdale** 1902
Oil on canvas, 101¼ x 56½ in.
National Gallery,
London

**William Merritt Chase,** 1902
Oil on canvas, 62½ x 41⅜ in.
The Metropolitan Museum of Art,
Gift of pupils of William M. Chase, 1905. (05.33)

**Theodore Roosevelt** 1903
Oil on canvas, 58½ x 40½ in.
US Naval Academy Museum,
New Haven, CT/Bridgeman Art Library, London

**An Artist in His Studio** c. 1903
Oil on canvas, 21½ x 28¼ in.
Charles Henry Hayden Fund,
Museum of Fine Arts,
Boston, MA

**Mrs. Fiske Warren (Gretchen Osgood) and Her Daughter Rachel** 1903
Oil on canvas, 60 x 40¼ in.
Gift of Mrs. Rachel Warren Barton and the Emily L. Ainsley Fund
Museum of Fine Arts,
Boston, MA

**Sir Frank Swettenham** 1904
Oil on canvas, 67¼ x 47½ in.
National Portrait Gallery,
London

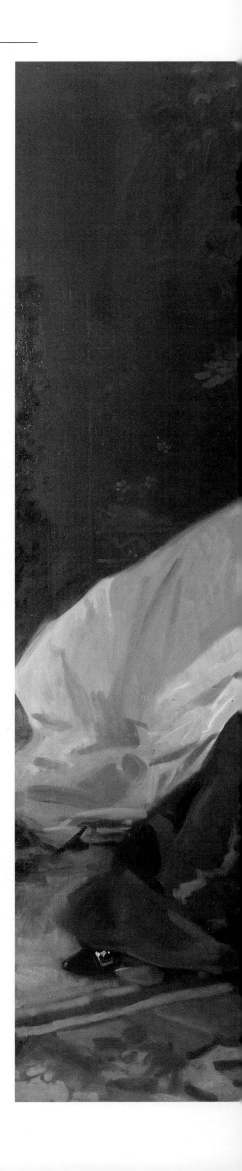

**The Misses Hunter** 1903
Oil on canvas.
Tate Gallery,
London

**The Black Brook** c. 1908
Oil on canvas, 21½ x 27½ in.
Tate Gallery,
London

**The Hermit (Il Solitario)** 1908
Oil on canvas, 37¾ x 38 in.
The Metropolitan Museum of Art,
Rogers Fund, 1911. (11.31)

**Mosquito Nets** 1908
Oil on canvas, 22¼ x 28¼ in.
Private Collection/Bridgeman Art Library, London

**Mountain Stream** 1910-12
Watercolor, wax and graphite on white wove paper, 13½ x 21 in.
The Metropolitan Museum of Art,
Purchase, Joseph Pulitzer Bequest, 1915. (15.142.2)

**Miss Eliza Wedgwood and Miss Sargent Sketching** 1908
Watercolour and graphite, 19¼ x 14 in.
Bequeathed by William Newall, 1922.
Tate Gallery,
London

**Reading** 1911
Watercolour on paper, 20 x 14 in.
The Hayden Collection
Museum of Fine Arts, Boston, MA

**Bringing Down Marble from the Quarries to
Carrara** 1911
Oil on canvas, 28⅛ x 36⅛ in.
The Metropolitan Museum of Art,
Harris Brisbane Dick Fund, 1917. (17.97.1)

**San Vigilio, Lago di Garda** c. 1913
Watercolor, 12⅝ x 21 in.
Tate Gallery,
London

**Henry James** 1913
Oil on canvas, 33½ x 26½ in.
National Portrait Gallery,
London

**Spanish Fountain** 1914
Watercolour and graphite on white wovepaper, 20⅞ x 13⁹⁄₁₆ in.
The Metropolitan Museum of Art,
Purchase, Joseph Pulitzer Bequest, 1915. (15.142.6)

**Tyrolese Interior** 1915
Oil on canvas, 28⅛ x 22¹⁄₁₆ in.
The Metropolitan Museum of Art,
George A. Hearn Fund, 1915. (15.142.1)

**Thou Shalt Not Steal** 1918
Watercolour on paper, 21 x 13¼ in.
Imperial War Museum, London/
Bridgeman Art Library, London

**Ruined Cathedral, Arras** 1918
Oil on canvas, 21½ x 2 ½ in.
Private Collection/Bridgeman Art Library, London

**Gassed** 1918-19
Oil on canvas, 90 x 240 in.
Imperial War Museum,
London

**The Interior of a Hospital Tent** 1918
Watercolor on paper, 15½ x 20¾ in.
Imperial War Museum,
London

**Isabella Stewart Gardner** 1922
Watercolour on paper, 16¾ x 12½ in.
Isabella Stewart Gardner Museum,
Boston, MA

**The Coming of the Americans to Europe** 1922
Oil on canvas, 176 x 73½ in.
Widener Library, Harvard University Art Museums,
Cambridge, MA

127

# ACKNOWLEDGEMENTS

The publisher is grateful to the following institutions for permission to reproduce the pictures on the pages noted below:

Armand Hammer Museum of Art: 38

In the Collection of The Corcoran Gallery of Art: 16, Gift of Miss Emily Sargent and Mrs. Violet Sargent Ormond,33

Calouste Gulbenkian Museum, Lisbon, Portugal: 60/1

Courtesy of Terra Museum of American Art, Chicago, IL: 65

Courtesy of the Flint Institute of Arts: 50

Courtesy the Trustees of the Public Library of the City of Boston: 17

Courtesy, Museum of Fine Arts, Boston, MA: 25(T), 27, 28/9, 31, 40/1, 76, 96/7, 98, 111

Des Moines Art Center: 36/37,

Fitzwilliam Museum, Cambridge, England: 22

Galleria degli Uffizi, Florence: 15

Isabella Stewart Gardner Museum, Boston, MA: 39, 88/9, 126

IWM, London: 23, 119, 122/3, 124/5

Jeu de Paume, Paris: 14

Los Angeles County Museum of Art: 75

Musée Franco-Americaine Blerancourt Chauny: 74

Musée Rodin, Paris: 51

Museum of Art, Rhode Island School of Design: 67

National Gallery, London 1, 93

National Gallery of Art, Washington, DC: 42/3

National Gallery of Scotland, Edinburgh: 79

National Museum of American Art/Art Resource,NY1 S0096289    80

National Portrait Gallery, London: 8, 25(B), 81, 99, 116

Royal Academy of Art, London: 82/3

© Photo Réunion des Musées Nationaux 9,14

Royal Geographical Society, London: 78

Sheffield City Art Galleries: 4, 52/3

Spencer Museum of Art: 45

© Sterling and Francine Clark Art Institute Williamstown, MA: 10, 34, 35

The Art Museum, Princeton University: 62

The Brooklyn Museum, New York: 68/9

The Harvard University Art Museums, Cambridge, MA: 12 (Gift of Mrs. Francis Ormond), (Gift of Mrs. Francis Ormond), 56 (Bequest of Grenville L. Winthrop), 127

The Metropolitan Museum of Art, N Y: 49, 54/5 and 77 (Gift of Mrs. Francis Ormond), 85, 87, 94, 104/5, 108/9, 112/3, 117, 118

The Minneapolis Institute of Arts: 58/9

The Pennsylvania Academy of Fine Arts, Philadelphia, PA: 48

The Sargent House Museum, Gloucester, MA. Gift of Emily Sargent: 6,7

The Taft Museum, Cincinnati, OH: 63

The Tate Gallery, London: 2, 13, 19, 20, 21, 32, 57, 64, 66, 72, 73, 84, 86, 92, 100/1, 102/3, 110, 114/5

US Naval Academy Museum, New Haven, CT: 95

via the Bridgeman Art Library: 15 (Galleria degli Uffizi), 26, 30, 44 (Private Collection), 46/7 (National Trust, London), 52/3 (Sheffield City Art Galleries), 64 (Tate Gallery, London), 68/9 (The Brooklyn Museum, New York), 70/1 (Private Collection), 74 (Musée Franco-Americaine/Giraudon), 78 (Royal Geographical Society, London), 79 (National Gallery of Scotland, Edinburgh), 82/3 (Royal Academy of Art, London), 86 (Tate Gallery, London), 90/1 (Private Collection), 95 (US Naval Academy Museum), 106/7 (Private Collection), 119 (IWM), 120/1 (Private Collection)